Flesh
The Greatest Sin

Eithne Strong

Attic Press
DUBLIN

First published by The Runa Press, 1980

British Library Cataloguing in Publication Data
Strong, Eithne
Flesh: The Greatest Sin
I. Title
823.914 [F]

ISBN 1-85594-083-3

Cover Design: Kate White
Origination: Verbatim Typesetting and Design
Printing: The Guernsey Press Co Ltd.

This book is published with the assistance of The Arts Council/An Chomhairle Ealaíon.

Dedication

To better understanding

Acknowledgements

Illustrations: Martina Leonard
                 Pete Richardson

About the Author

Eithne Strong, poet in Irish and English, is also a fiction writer. A varied life includes taking a university degree after family rearing, participating in publishing, freelance journalism, teaching, work with the media, co-ordinating creative writing courses, giving readings of her work widely and representing Irish writing in Europe—Denmark, France, Germany, Finland—in England, the USA and Canada. She has been awarded travel bursaries. Her work appears in many anthologies. She is a member of the executive committee of the Irish Writers' Union.

Born in West Limerick, she has lived for many years in Dublin where she was married, had nine children and was widowed. She has been involved with the mentally disabled—her youngest son has a mental disability.

Thirteen of Eithne Strong's books have been published.

I

Tom Regan schoolmaster, — fine man, they said —
did not really like God
but prayed most fiercely every day,
eyes shut, brow greaved,
following desperately
prescription to Heaven;
he also to the letter
followed the doctor's instruction
against apoplexy:
Thomas required rigid pronouncements
to hold a surging panic
regarding energy.

What were his driving forces? Not always
clear but certainly it was of first importance
to be safe, to keep a civil distance,
not to get mixed up with the neighbours.
A civil distance was the desirable;
titanic rage, *that* had to be watched:
murder, splitting heads with spades —
that had to be watched; allowed only
so far the sudden mallet fist, raised
but not falling, or the purple bellow
constrained to civilised vocabulary:
'Don't offer to give me cheek... '

Thomas remembered constantly, vividly, that he
was terrified of not making it to Heaven.
Because of such perpetual recollection
he put iron around flesh, the betrayer:
flesh that had to do with ketching in cowhouses,
slopping in ditches, that meant knickers,
odours that frightened with the pull of temptation.

Flesh was Hell; keep it inflexibly bound;
let loose instead to the mountain, the gun, the bog,
the dog; tramp wickedness out
of the flesh; weary it out through Barneigue,
up Knockfinisk, on to Rooskagh; to exhaustion plague
the slimy demon. Meet only the men.
Go fishing with the men. There is safety
with the men — women did not shoot nor fish
barring the few that you wouldn't get within
an ass's roar of them, the ones aping county —
shopkeepers' daughters in white figured breeches
riding hunters around Newcastle West and Rathkeale.

Beware the raging fire.
Get to Heaven.
Be safe, avoid temptation:
keep off the drink — one drop
fatal for the *dúchas* is in the blood.
Walk off the urges,
height after glen, tramp on tramp —
the rivers keep flooding,
the mountain is endless.

He didn't remember his mother. His sister Mary Kate
was always there. She liked the outside air
and did not talk much, stirring meal for pigs,
for hens chopping cosherwawn; chop chop chop
on the old grey board near the gravel pile,
green hopping bits that the lunatic fowl chased;
her fingers were forever stained brown from the juice.
Their father liked fair days; he went with Quirk,
his cousin and bosom pal. They had come from Kerry,
the two, and with their own hands had built homes,
getting stones and sand from the near quarry;
the kiln they made which burned the blue stones white.
A right pair of boyos, the father and Quirk, in local
estimation, which meant they held their drink, came out
smart in a deal, were never bested for an answer;
Quirk might grab a collop when he had a few jorums,
the leg might screech, You dirty oul divil you,
and wish him younger: he had a way with his drunken paw.

Tom Regan wished himself like ribald parent and pal
but his head was always fraught with Hell —
how could *they* forget it?
Or were their antics just bravado?
Dumb, he stayed, not a syllable aloud.
Mary Kate spoke nothing either
to father, cousin, brother, but
watching the heavy bull
over the bounds
was subject to uncomfortable titter.

The same boyos had been through the Land Campaign;
in the next glen a ruined house stood still, still kept
the name, Campaign, since the time when they and others
in the district held there, strong, through thick and thin.

Young Regan heard the talk
standing around the forge,
Paddy the Smith sizzling horses' hooves —
his helper chewed the parings — talk
holding up the churchyard wall
Sunday mornings,
afternoons, the hurling match,
the snug in Togher's, nights
when the hard men shot long spits
in sputtering ashes under Ned Togher's
boiling spuds.

Old Regan dropped dead
one day while his son
was pedalling back
the eighteen daily miles
from teaching job
in a further parish.
In spite of being on the right side
of the canon, a while yet
to wait for favour of post
at the local school, Cloneen.

                  Death, and other things
cause vacancies: the Tans in lorries
tore around the country daily,
pot shots at anything that moved.
Mary Kate stood stock still in the bog,
brown on brown, and stayed alive.
Tom Regan, now local schoolteacher, with a bit
of land, had to hire a man to run it;
Mary Kate still had full domestic possession
until her brother, caging Hell, brought in Ellen.

II

Ellen orphan, knew nuns as her beginning.
They make their own beeswax. Orphans polished
convent floors, two by two, left to right swing swing,
on their knees with the wide thick rags before them;
miles of shining convent corridors for the exemplification
of cleanliness next to godliness and for visiting
importances like the occasional canon, oftener inspector,
very rare archbishop. Ellen was not hungry, getting bread —
and jam on Sundays; and rosaries were constant diet,
Hail Mary, Holy Mary. Purest of the pure, Mary:
everyone is to know the awful need for purity.
House of Gold pray for us. Tower of Ivory.

How a Mary a house of gold?
Silence!
How does a tower of ivory pray?
Hold your tongue!
Do what you're told!
No one understands everything.
Never *never* offend the Immaculate Conception.
What does conceived without sin mean?
Isn't it plain — it means what it says.

The Terrible Sins are those against purity;
the vilest. Remember the sixth commandment
Thou shalt not commit adultery.
What is adultery? Hold your tongue
and learn obedience. Mortify the flesh,
that is the enemy; not to be pampered,
scourge it that you may not fall into eternal fire.

Remember what it is like to be burned. Imagine
your whole body burning and never any ending.
Imagine that punishment and realise then how much better
to punish yourself now; polish harder, go hungrier;
be glad you are cold; cold and purity combine;
welcome the sweat of heavy labour, it washes you pure;
remember purity is supreme; to be virgin
there is nothing higher for a woman.

Mystic Rose, pray for us.
What is a Mystic Rose?
Silence.
Remember the constant use of control.
All born into this Vale of Tears carry the sin,
the original weakness of Eve and Adam.

We pay the price of their indulgence.
Eve gave in, encouraged another to the flesh,
We must refuse; do not lean back in your chair,
stretch flesh to the last endurance.
Remember Christ stretched on Calvary.
Drive it; remember Christ driven under the cross.
Christ scourged; scourge the flesh. Chasten it.
Indulgence heats the blood. Chastity is everything,
Deny the self. Do not look in mirrors —
what have you to see but your vain self that is dust.
Do not taste. Remember Christ had gall and vinegar.
Do not touch. Remember the Seven Deadly sins.
Live for the Day of Judgement when the flesh
that has been kept pure will rise again.
Deny! Deny! — for purity on Judgement Day!

                  Ellen, orphan, knew the sound
of lonesome bells in the hellish dark, and whispered
rushing prayers into the rasping rime of institutional grey
blankets. Sister Benignus creaked Heavenwards
in blockety elastic boots down entombed miles
of polished corridors to her coffin cell.

Taught to teach tomorrow
what she learned today
Ellen, orphan,
product of edicts
denials, spartan procedures,
was finally dispatched
on the sacred word
of Father Downey P.P.
to instruct girls
in the district of Cloneen,
where Thomas,
on Government pay,
was giving his hourly whack
at ignorance.

III

Now, Ellen, previous denizen of dormitories,
slept alone above the country pub.
Below her, beer one side, the other
anything from pin to pike,
from cotton spool to bale of hemp,
hair-oil cockly coloured blue and gold
and purple for the quiffs of local cocks
at crossroad dances Sunday nights,
'Indian' corn, orange-rich shiny ovals for hens,
for humans, crushed to yellow luscious diet, filling fat
the sack below the rolled down rim against which balanced
crazily the huge tin scoop to measure out this yalla male,
the dead-fine-male of local parlance. Women baked it;
the general taste spoke out in praise of yalla bread.

Three miles to school, all weathers, children walked
in their welcome motley — Pasadena patching Syracuse —
yet emigrant help withal, often no winter shoes
(bare summer feet were general), drenchings; wet layered
on fireguard; smells of sooty clothes; bodies; drying urine.
The parish priest said 'Turf', so they brought
sods under oxter and the odd assload, soon pelted fast
behind the red half-wall in the porch where draggled
ragged coats. Fleas in turf. Boys jeering girls,
doing the dirty, sneaking sods. If a man had sons
and no daughter, he brought his load
for the boys' fire only. Turf meant fights.

Out in the yard at the higher end, the WCs,
sited for slope, visible to the nation,
stone and winter-cold, two holes in horizontal wood
at either side the listening wall; rude
hygiene, share to share for young and staff.
In wishful dignity, need to urgent defecation
simulated an ambulatory look at nature and set off
guffaws in passing creamery carts, cracks on the condition
of teachers' bowels. Stuff piled up in summer stench.
Ellen, early orphan, had a sensitive stomach.
Suffer for Christ, suffer smell, the Voices said,
for the sake of the crucified Christ.

Yap, the said, yap-yap. Red setters and a stone-grey
house. Out of the far dark they came, the western dark.
Thomas, assistant master in the schoolhouse of Cloneen;
Master Ford, Principal. The two did not agree.
The red dogs had long faces, the dogs of Master Ford,
that Thomas liked but not their owner. In the schoolhouse
he kept uncivil distance; in the school a long hate
lived, the masters hating. The older man — clever,
they said, wasted in the bogs, they said — jealous.
When driven knowledge got nowhere in the brains of boys
from backward places, Master Ford heck-hecked narrow mouth
of spite, indirect and lethal, about things to do with

dimwit fools, their fathers, mothers, yankee cousins
or uncles in the RIC. Thomas used a different way,
satire being too cerebral for his pounding frustrations.
The mountain road heard his bellowing rage from
school summer windows; boys wet their pants.
He flailed his mallet fist, worked teeth;
'D'you see that?' first aloft, 'then don't offer
to defy me.' Defy, in this category, meaning
insult with ignorance; the boys in terrified pants
would never defy. 'Yap,' Mrs Ford to Ellen in the girls'
school, 'yap. Mrs Dunne is on the way again. No restraint,
Mike Dunne. And seven already. An animal.'

The master's dogs bitched twice a year. The oldest
reddest one had white hairs round her eyes, her tits
slacked to the ground. Old broken thing, Mrs Ford said.
Mike Dunne, she said, was like the gombeen's bull
that was kept in the near field by the road,
quicker serve that way. You couldn't object,
no use anyway; what did the gombeen care? You couldn't
name the thing the bull was doing but you could see,
and call the girls in from watching at the wall.

While Mrs Ford
declared inside the school,
outside, by the mountain road
where roars from Thomas crashed
the newcome cobbler opened shop,
shoed the countryside,
touched — pant pant —
imagination of the breasting sixth;
the brazen biggest one he told
You'd dhraw wather from it.
she had a jaw for talk
and talked the sweating panting class
her twisted run of men and women,
her steaming store
from yabbering guilty sheds
and barns and hearths.

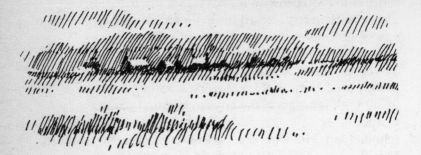

Thomas married Ellen.
Maintaining perpetual hate, Master Ford
and Thomas corroded one the other
from diametric rostrums.
Mary Kate, till now domestic boss,
was not to welcome in another woman.
Two disparate women in one house
was not to work
'Twill have to be,' said Ellen,
'that Mary Kate gets matched
and settled outside the place.'
said Ellen, newly close to country ways
and quick to graft. A match was made.

IV

It was a good farm, east county, but
a place where was, oddly, still a blight
of women: old mother, daft sister, unyoung
furtive husband, mad for a ketch — a glut
of thighs, juice, fistfuls of female yield.
Mary Kate, lean, locked, was not happy.
Very soon she began to die a little,
each day, diminishing little by little.

Husband, old witch mother, half-mad sister —
they did not know about this dying;
clamped in their own travail, they
could not see, not read what ailed
this new specimen.

Whenever he took her — pony-trap —
to town, she wordlessly looked
for signs of her home district, west:
someone with creel of turf, load of rushes
from 'the place behind'; she pined
for a trace of 'the people back'.
Separated from them, forgetting almost
how enmities could, used to, divide,
she invested enshrined remembrances
with tribal exaltation: her people, her kind.

'The people east' were an alien breed.
Hard to say exactly what made them so.
Someway, she felt, their difference had to do
with owning big fields, knowing nothing
about the ways of turf, burning only coal,
having orchards — in the bogs, fruit trees did not fruit.
This eastern part was called the Golden Vale:
she hated it. On it grain plumped,
cattle fattened, farmers thrived.
She hated it.

Standing on a wall in one field, on certain days,
she could see an empty hill in her own country.
She went often to this field and looked west
to that hill, lifting out of the bogland. Such land
had been her life; that stark far curve became,
of necessity, her conjured consolation.
Turned to it, she saw itself no more but,
rather, standing there on stone, felt
the rich thick ooze of bog between toes;
the round, the red, the squelch, the pink, the jade
of moss under feet; legs were to the knee in splurge;
legs now galloping, caked in turfy drying juice;

flying skirt now madly drenched in the amber splash;
hands, scrambling to a bank, were grasping clumps
of strong fionawn, rejoicing in their springy green
russeting from the tip; fingers were crushing,
nose breathing the incomparable myrtle. Standing so,
she did not feel the immediate air above her husband's
                                    fields,
heavy with smells of local growth (for her starvingly rich)
but felt instead wind from far Slieve Callan, as on
her father's land, Shannon between; and saw,
not level grain-filled fields but a longed-for
nourishing bleakness of moor and the distant rise
of Moher blurring the sky above Liscannor.

She was afraid of the old woman in the house, black
witch's headcloth, small fierce eye. When the third
child miscarried that was when Mary Kate left
her husband's house one day in a fever. He was
with his successful crops; the other women
in their separate retreats; tick-tock the clock,
silent afternoon. The crazy sister prayed a lot:
Hail Mary, Holy Mary, rocking in her room. No one
saw Mary Kate go. She just mazed from her sick bed;
a day later was found crawling westwards, her sodden
cotton nightdress in tatters. They buried her
in the east however — the husband's cemetery plot:
                                    good growing ground.

V

Ellen, orphan, teacher,
inheritor
of multiple
religious riches,
long since wife
to Tom Regan
and now expanded
variously
in the married state,
enjoying the push
of dual power,
house and school.

Pegeen (hired girl) when you are making the beds
don't forget what I told you about catching fleas:
the way to nab them is to turn back the top
of the blanket, inch by inch — they stay stuck
in the wool where the heat is;
if you give the bedclothes too sudden a jerk
they'll make a big hop
and that'll be the last you'll see of them.
Now remember to crush their heads
between your thumbnails. I'm plumb
sure there are some for didn't I notice
a bite on Shamie's neck...

and let me see yourself . . . lift up your chin, girl!
Aren't those bites I see on you? Mother of God,
girl, you're riddled. So hurry up, will you, go
after them the way I say. And you know
what I told you about emptying the slops —
rinse out the jerries with the wash water
from the basins in the rooms, and after,
when you empty the bucket, be sure to fling
far back in the manure heap
for decency's sake.

Shameen, look here!
I've stirred your cod-liver oil —
go on, drink it, no dawdling...
you know well we have to hurry to school. Yes, Shameen,
we'll be walking; no coddling in ponytraps. Isn't it feet
that are fine and strong the Lord gave you and your sister,
Nance? You should be grateful for the use of strong limbs.
Thomas, go and tell that idler, Paud, what he should be at
for the day. And Pegeen, you're not to be having that
fellow in the house when we're gone; give him his dinner
and pack him off out again. He never does all he should
be doing outside; bone lazy, always ready to shove
into the fire — and all that topdress to fling,
those drains to dig, that litter to spread — outside
for him: *I'll* even talk to him myself before we leave.

Be sure now, girl,
be sure to sweep down; get at those cobwebs today.
And about the dinner, well,
there's that bit of mutton from yesterday —
keep that for the master; the doctor says
the salt is bad for his pressure. Mash
the few potatoes for the children's pandy; use
the end of the butter, don't touch the new
I made yesterday evening — keep that
for the master; it'll have to last
yet awhile with only the one cow milking
these days. Thomas! Thomas?

D'you hear me?
Ah sure, what's the use asking you?
I, that was never bred to it, know more
about the farm than any of ye; Pegeen
take a look there at the back of the calendar:
what are the dates we wrote down
for this season's calving? I'd make a better farmer
than any of ye, and I from the town;
if only I were a man
I'd put in a harder span
than anyone. Thomas, d'you hear? Hurry on, Thomas,
there might well be an inspector behind before us.

So went Ellen, day in, out, into the bitter weather.
On Thomas! Children on! into the day.
Run on. Hurry on. It's good for you to run.
What do you want with ponytrap? Coddlers!
Paud has plenty to occupy him for us not to be
taking him from his work, tackling a pony
to drive us a stone's throw; ready enough is he
for distraction; by the time he'd get that animal
untackled again 'tis no work he'd do.
Her high leather boots attacked the road,
crunched through ice; her small head
in its closetough hat, cut against the wind and won.

The east wind was her bitter foe;
she talked of it as though it stalked her,
waiting to knife. Sometimes it stabbed her low,
her breathing lacerated. She organised
strategies against it, announcing tactics
to the family. It was a diabolic,
disembodied force that was a relief to hate
without fear of the commandments.
What does fear do to flesh? One other
feared enemy (what does fear do?) was less
assailable: the Church was on its side
calling it Conjugal Right.

Angrily confused was she before this foe.
From the first, Voices of Authority had forbidden:
Deny flesh: Mortify. Abnegate. Voices had wrought
fear: Remember Hell. Remember Mary, the Immaculate,
conceived *without sin*. Remember. Ellen
remembered that flesh was sin, flesh laid on flesh brought
stirrings that meant Hell. The old voices sounded always
unrelentingly in her life. Do not indulge. Punish.
Crucify self. And the new: from the pulpit, now,
the priest frenzied out his loathing; vituperation
of the flesh convulsed him near seizure.

At night

he searched bushes
long grass, ditches,
torch and stick flesh — flash.
He howled he would exterminate impurity;
his duty to insist how putrid the body,
how easily the devil's. He, God's annointed,
ordained to work for the purest Virgin,
would not, he screamed, could not,
rest, where sinful horrors stank.
He battered all the courting nooks;
no couples met unknown.

Long since terrorised to non-response, flesh
of Ellen could not accommodate to this unwelcome licence
called Conjugal Right: it established her bewilderment,
recoil, hate, but never joy; an insidious
antagonist, it swelled her with pregnant ills,
weighed thick her ankles, but it was
ecclesiastically endorsed, Church backed,
and Ellen lived Church-awed.
Confusion gave her a lashing tongue so that
scorn became her general reflex
to every sign of the allowed act,
Yet the enemy took access; it was the law.

And she conceived with no rejoicing. Five times.
The two who lived she reared with all respect
to received authority; they must be primed
against the coils of flesh, made know the body should
be fed only for work to be done, not for gratification;
her scorn spat the vileness of men, the grossness, lust:
'...and haven't we heard what to do about scandal? pluck
out the eye, cut off the hand — clear enough, isn't it?
Where there is the bad drop, a man starts with that taint;
he ought to keep an iron clamp on the blood;
people with the bad drop take a filthy satisfaction,
using their wives with Conjugal Right.'

She spewed her contempt on self-indulgent ancestors,
grandfathers, uncles, cousins. Whenever possible
she talked with women, low secret colloquies
to do with tumours, wombs, female parts not to be named
before men: exclusive privacies uttering miscarriages,
haemorrhages, unending press of pregnancies
loaded with moan, with women's rage at their abuse.
In living dread, however, of a vengeful Maker,
they always deluged speech with God-be-praised,
named His saints, called on His mother,
wishfully protected, by this summoned phalanx
of sanctity, from eternally punishable blasphemy.

All was God's will; how, then, place demanding men?
They were a different thing. Dilemma. Ellen
arranged, for her satisfaction, a public placebo:
relishing her cronies' rage, she, contrarily,
did not, abroad, indict her man; what she
held legitimate pride required it must be thought
she had the best; to impress, therefore, amid
the women, the scope of her domain, she fabricated
many a subterfuge, mostly doing so well that
she believed her own deceit. Pride — this kind,
she did not rate as one of the Seven Deadly —
was to her imperative, a sort of personal oxygen.

She gave, then, to be known
that Thomas, her Tom, was
exemplary, 'good', meaning
'never looking for any of *that*'
the baneful cause of other women's woes.
Her various pains and aches
she would attribute publicly
to reasons different from theirs,
keeping for domiciled fury
the verbal annihilation
that always met
any rearing signs in Tom.

As for him,
his parts lifted no more;
banished
from speech, sight, touch,
to an eliminatory limbo,
never again to gain
even a grudging scope.
Whenever
bombardments shattered,
or even threatened,
Thomas always
took to the moor.

The moor was his part-renewal.
There the ancient and forever things
comforted. As monks retreat to cells
Thomas turned to old sights, sounds, smells:
heather, cannawawn, the rush of wind on face and neck,
meadowsweet belly-high by the ditch,
the sudden gowreen roe splatting from a pool;
and, most of all, the curlew-cry stirred
in him some deep part that sent an answering
lonely sound. Spreading, it seemed, illimitably,
composite of numberless blends, the reidh
offered harmony to his fissured state.

VI

What progeny could issue from such convoluted
                              beginnings?
Inside the womb of Ellen sperm met egg.
A long poison, still virulently strong
from the past of flayings, witches, burnings,
went into that fusion.
The helpless embryo passively received its legacy
of fear, intersticed through the cankered being. (What does
fear do to flesh that should be spirit's blossoming?)
The old Voices of Authority always ruled in Ellen;
oddly, they did not condemn pride of place
but declared to be Hell pride in flesh:
her daughter, Nance, must from the first be cauterised.

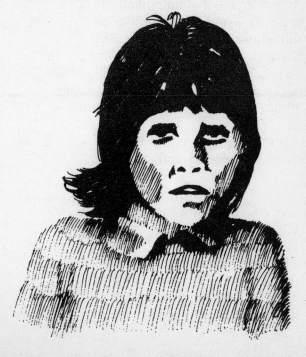

To prevent sin
this girl must be
made to see herself ugly.
Ah, your shape
'tis pitiful,
lank, thin,
nothing to be proud of;
and isn't it you that brought
the sallow skin:
dead spit of your cracked aunt,
Mary Kate — God rest her . . .

but sure 'tis a blessing
to be ugly:
you're better off
than to be
always preening —
that leads to mortal sin.

Flesh, the corruptible mould that grows on bones,
the particularly dangerous outgrowth on chest,
ingrowth between legs — that unthinkable lurk
impossible to purify — must, because
of intrinsic sulliedness, be purged incessantly.
Fear drove Ellen:
'What are you doing with your hand, you filthy thing!
Take your hand out of your knickers; go and wash;
go and scour your disgusting hands this minute.'
Drove Thomas:
'Don't tell a lie! If I ever catch you at that
filth, I'll break every bone in your body.'

                     Guilt grew with Nance,
outgrowing her, going through and all about her.
The Voices, active in Ellen, mother,
continued in the child,
sounding the maxims, endorsing:
body is evil; given to rottenness, unregenerate,
needing ever severest curbs if not to drag
the soul to doom. Nance had a healthy nature;

in her life was strong; pulls drew her
and then the Voices forbade. Urges to touch,
explore body-self, enjoy sensation, were blackest
evil, mortal sin, everlasting fire.

A visiting cousin
showed her in the heather;
already at six
she had done the Terrible Thing;
he, sixteen, size of a man,
size of her father —
once, slipping in the sea,
wildly she had grabbed
the place on her father;
afterwards
the remembered clutch
was shameful.

                The big cousin, using his own,
showed the play of hand he wished. Held, drawn,
palpitating urge inside her, she did as asked.
Afterwards guilt engulfed:
all dark powers closed in
upon a fearful night-loneliness.
And yet, repeated climax
for this man-boy (and her new excitement
that surely was deepest sin)
held day-time sway; many times the act.
He went. She was six.

At school, Ellen and curate prepared the young
for First Confession. Thus, newly catalogued,
Nance heard incomprehensible diagnosis of sinful terrain.
Thou shalt not commit adultery; body is treacherous
to soul; soul is to be reached only by mortifying
body. What is mortify? Kill. Kill the flesh
that the soul can live. Thou shalt not commit adultery.
What is adultery? Most shameful thing. And then, red silence.
No further explaining; there was to be no plain speaking,
but, to cover the livid pause, further decrying generalities
on fleshly sins against the Sixth Commandment:
body always lowers; can destroy soul. A fight to death.

Adultery —
this must be
what she had done:
six years old
and a filthy sinner.
Yet words would not come, she knew no bravery
to shape confession. Night was worst: should she die
. . . there gaped the caverns of endless burning.
Fear reared out of the dark. Courage nowhere.
Nor anyone she could tell. Six years old, hiding
the heavy secret. Expounded punishments did not combine
to courage; and now it was Confession Day.

                    Small church of stone.
Ellen, orphan that was, teacher, mother; now importantly
sibilant, shepherding children to the confessional;
amid this latest bunch her child, Nance, a life unknown
inside the unremarkable head and sallow skin that sealed
young bewildered flesh. How tell a priest the monstrous
                                  thing
when all could hear? — Confession, sacrament of secrecy,
but Nance could hear stiff whispers of Confiteor, prescribed
Hail Marys and Latin absolution. How tell? How...? and now
                    'Anything else, child?'
Oh yes, oh agonising yes . . . but she did not tell.

The old priest's bulbous nose hulked gloomily
behind the grille; her mother and all outside
to know the shame…! she left the box fouler sinner —
hadn't they been told? — crime of sacrilege
(hadn't they been told?) laid on the already damning load.
The next day, First Communion. White. To signify
stainlessness (they had been told). Ellen always
had dubbed her ugly; in this deliberate white
Nance queerly felt mocked, bony knees, lank hair, despised
skin; but greatest mock was black black soul inside
the white. After Mass, Thomas gave her a half-crown:
immense riches; a neighbour said, 'The little innocent.'

They took
her picture by the church:
small girl, tight mouth, dropped head,
An ugly thing, me,
with a damned soul.
And yet
she had a kind
of sideways hopeless hope:
maybe, maybe . . .
the photo might show pretty;
soul might not be black;
hell-fear might not tonight terrify . . .

Courage did not come.
Months passed and it was winter.
The bogs stretched sere.
Years went and it was summer;
swallows curved; larks rang pure.
In school and out,
Nance learned
plenty extracurricular information
having nothing to do with class but much
with coorts, doing it, bulls, ditches,
witchy midwives, bloody births, women, men
— all this from mixed oral sources:

no dearth of racing older tongues
from huddled playground knots, tittering boreens,
and hunched Pegeen in the kitchen when Ellen was out.
In the kitchen Pegeen squarked at Paud who,
well understanding what juice she craved, gave none;
this maddened her whose obvious pangs he gloated on;
he, therefore, got his twisted way which was to goad
a manless women, and she got nothing but madder.
Later they put her in the County Asylum.
So, Nance learned — and then longed
for a great warm receiving of her distorted load,
her heavy sin. The weight had grown

for, according to rule, performing the ritual
of regular confession, she had never confessed;
thus (hadn't they been told?) she was continually
weighting mortal sin on mortal sin. Hourly
was she reminded of the chasmed peril; lived
a jolting swing between opposed places,
one being all that pounding terror conjured,
the other — haunted escape — being where bog things
were happy, river ran, birds sang, the mountain blessed,
where sky domed, books entranced, there was
deliciousness for tea; Ellen existed.

That Ellen should be was of the essence; daughter
worshipped mother; hated her; with great need
required her; repudiated her in fluent scorn:
daughter's pendulum need of total mother. Ellen being less
than whole (who is whole?), early orphaned, having known
as mother institutional figures only, had patterns none
else by which to shape her mother's self. Made to heed
in youth the iron hand, she used like method
with this uncertain child, while Nance longed
for great receiving warmth, soft all-holding sureness
into which she could precipitate her churning moil
of too-soon knowledge. Could such be found in Ellen?

Long wishfulness engendered shivering tiny hope,
begot some shaking courage that *did* turn Nance to Ellen,
(Tom at the time was on the moor, Shamus high in mountain;
it was a Sunday afternoon of yellow velvet smells,
the gorse being full; Ellen upright on a garden ledge
taking legitimate time with the Country Travelling Library
— The Elusive Picaroon, fantastical but decorous)
no flooding rush but stammered shamed limpings
to which the mother gave what seemed as rigid marble edge,
not looking once from book on lap
as Nance crawled sweating syllables. So mother was direly
struck
to silent shock; so daughter was not received.

But peculiarly
the crippled telling helped a healing second.
From the blank that was Ellen's incapacity
grew in Nance her own quavering self-promise,
a further hurting urge:
after Saturday piano in the town
she ran the suffocating thump to market church
where, maybe, fewer knowing nudges
or even none — oh longing hope — and so got told
at last the long telling; got walked,
before the town and country mix of shaming eyes,
the impossible walk from the priest's box.

Momentous day.
The strongest,
highest she had known;
decided
out of herself alone.
That was the releasing point:
this power of decision.
Her mind sang,
she, racing the streets;
the grey town river
flashed sungold.
She was ten.

VII

As had been for the mother
so it would be for her child:
Ellen decided —
Thomas getting token consultation —
and chose for her reasons
the boarding school (Faithful Followers of Jesus),
results being the thing:
firsts in Ireland
for Inter and Leaving;
keep up with, get beyond
the gombeen's girls
now doing famously in the Civil Service.

Sisters in religion, amalgam of women,
Faithful Followers from the general
texture of Irish provincial life — no high blood
since Kinsale? — daughters of farms, shops,
professions; a dowry meant choir rank,
lack of it, lay function:
baking bread, chicken feeding;
no matter, it was all a vocation —
or was it? a calling?
Perhaps so; from sources enigmatic
something perhaps called to pursue
a life of relative restriction.

Good women and chaste, the Faithful Followers;
for some — maimed leg, hairy face, cleft palate —
the convent meant refuge a raw world refused.
Assumption of the nunly garb, being visible announcement
of elected celibacy, was equally circumvention
of the pain of spurning; rejection was thus forestalled.

Chaste women and good, according to their view
which inescapably was that particular perspective
theirs through heritage; therefore since they knew
no candid speech about the body they could speak none.
Areas of anatomy could be judiciously discussed,
even diagrammed.

                        Necessary of course to stop
before the anus, the precise character of which
was never delineated, the mention of this egress
to the outer world being totally taboo.
A pupil might wonder — in fear
since it must be sin to think on such a base quarter —
what was the official term for that part ignored
in proper conversation yet snigger-told as hole
in stolen dirty stories, might wonder and never hear.
Present and possible future functions of other parts,
specially and terrifyingly female, rendered them
of such excruciating embarrassment
as not to be even peripherally suggested.

Girls then, grew for the purpose of being pure,
and of passing exams into banks, filing systems.
Trade with the Lord: I'll be good, forego pleasure,
do the Nine Fridays, so let me win. In this school,
not as in the mountain one, clustered girls did not
insinuate the banned, the steaming secret flesh.

A different cast these, less rawly throbbing;
less ravenous for shreds of meaty lore.
Where questioning was, it was dumb,
there being tacit blank beyond particular signs.
Nuns recognised the existence only of fathers, brothers;
the subject of boyfriend was significantly ignored.

Good women, the Faithful Followers. Diligent.
They instructed the young unsparingly.
No lazy nuns. Work, a high ideal.
Rigour, the example. Instruction went
into many things but the body sexual.
was not one. The insistent nonexistent.

Even the Retreat priest did not dare. He whom,
through days of total silence
girls in their wishfulness
imagined saint, investing him
with sanctity, worshipping their own hunger,
he, from his white removed celibacy, warned:
girls, who are differently composed, must not rouse,
must not tempt beyond his strength the weak male;
a man should be helped to avoid the lightning
of his nature, not be ignited by idle tantalising.
Poor pitiable man left helpless
by Adam's ease with Eve.

Monk wept, dwelling on the purity unparalleled
of the spotless Virgin; her virtue wrought him to tears.
The girls were awed to witness
such testimony of holiness. He was a saint,
they said when emerged from the silence of Retreat.
They said it to their Saturday regular confessor
who laughed, they felt, irreverently;
they did not like this profane noise
which mocked their private breathless shrine where
was the imagined priest,
their wishful sign
of attained earthly purity.

For Nance, fifteen, such emphasised stainlessness,
this emotional eloquence of the mission priest
meant returned upheaval; convulsions
of renewed recoil before remembered putrescence.
Peace so agonisedly won, was cleft; a plague
of scruples smote her adolescent state,
gnawing every wracked moment. At night,
the others asleep, she spread herself as crucified
on the freezing floor beside her bed. Expiation
had to continue. Arduously she increased
punitive strainings, new attempts at holiness
in the manner of saints' lives, continually read.

She knew yearnings for stigmata, spiritual flagellations,
mystic exaltation. Through denial fulfilment;
enjoyment is the lesser way; *the* way, one of sorrow,
crucifixion. Suffering has prior place, not chiefly
for what it here achieves in chastening flesh, will,
making malleable what is obdurate, but for greater state
in Heaven. Delight deferred for its ultimate increase.
Atonement had anew to be for now again
a new doubt lacerated: her momentous confession
made through such wrenched effort at age ten
had been at fault. Over and over,
in exacerbation of spirit, she sought to recreate
the pattern of that once-thought triumphant feat.

Impossible now to get the sequence of that telling,
five years gone, to the required exactitude.
Confessing, now, was not her difficulty. She longed
and longed to spill, each week tell over and again
the same obsessive points. Sick with the disease
of the fixed idea. 'A lack of faith,' the confessor —
chaplain to the school, a man of rule, not partial
to adolescent fog — pronounced. 'You are contrite.
You have confessed. You have not repeated the sins.
You must believe you are forgiven.'
The emotive priest who wept
was more to her taste than this clipped brusquerie.

Yet this newly presented view of faith
stood ground. Gradually
a wished belief began its cure:
the acceptance of forgiveness.
But stronger than ever previously,
revulsion against flesh, the corrupting burden.

At seventeen a glimpse of compromise, she being candidate
for Child of Mary. In the school code it was imperative
to achieve such rank the final year: pinnacle of local height,
of peculiarly compelling point, thrustingly used
as blackmail by the convinced sisterhood:
If you are not so, or so, you will not receive it.
To be refused was deep disgrace; the cloud of exclusion
blackened into the future; one left school condemned.
The day of bestowal was marked by a competitive white dress,
ritual and feast. Nance took part, while seeing dress, and feast
as compromise. Greatness meant abnegation.
She judged the nuns, her friends, herself as mediocre breed.

Nuns needed nuns; some prim canvassing went on
in the final months: 'We have been watching
your disposition. We feel you have the qualities
to be developed for God… in *our* Order, that is.'
Visiting nuns from missionary orders were received
with reserved courtesy, allowed access to classes
so as to deliver their recruiting appeal.
Afterwards, they being safely gone, pupils
were delicately enjoined to note
that charity begins at home.
For Nance, inevitable self-questioning:
What should I…? Could I…? Shall I…?

55

VIII

School left behind now;
options for the future.
Severe in-looking.
Will I be,
could I be
nun?
As Thomas, her father,
in stress
turned to the moor,
so Nance searched the bogland;
decisions were demanded:
then tramp and traipse the heights and glens.

He that loses his life . . . but it must be utter loss
no halfway nuns plumfeeding on mediocrity.
She despised the well-fed middleness which seemed
to her such life, neither one nor other thing,
the hankering between world and out-of-it
that appeared the mode of Faithful Followers
and their ilk. Contempt only for that compromise.
If she went, it would be to stark extreme;
to fasting, abrasive cloth, erupted skin, immolation,
hourly honing of the flesh. Should she go
she would make departure absolute;
between selected way and world, irrevocable rift.

The contemplative way.
It of utter silence.
Goodbye. Close the grille.
Vision of self ennobled to mystic elevation.
But yet need for close scrutiny of such,
pride with lust equally deadly amid the Seven

She searched for decision which curiously came
in the henhouse doorway. It had been a day
of sharp hard showers. Out of the grey
twisting glens loneliness followed. Sky
hung pale over evening cold. Grudging summer.
Out of the dripping shrubs three pines rose black,
like dark of ages. Between her and the treeless bog
these three figured the hard chill sky, insisting
resolution. She crouched in the henhouse door,
hearing fowls quark misery; twilight unrest
of limboed hens (soon the knife);
Loneliness lived; hen-smell of old dung hung alchemised.

And then, decision:
from the profane altar
between hens and pines
rose sacrificial act of mind
to the Good, but —
she would not be nun.

Healthy body; eager. Flesh that must be used for good
only. Swimming. Yes. Good. Climbing, hiking —
things allowable, comprehensible, thought of freely.
But that Other Thing . . . peripherally Nance allowed
the sickening scene that pressed continually at invasion;

the briefest image only was bearable; her body
partner in that deed licensed by virtue of marriage
— such coupling could only be for the duty of it;
the Church decree for procreation.
She would, if called on, suffer it for duty's sake
as, had she taken the nun-role she would have borne
daily denial or the leper touch.

Yet, already, every particle
in present and future flesh petrified to resist
such necessity. Passionately she wished
the energy conjoining women and men
to involve mind only;
cleanness lay that way,
excitement but no taint: this could be
the intense clear union. Yes, mind
was quintessential; marriage should
centre on that. Mind, therefore, she sought
in men; idealising, in her needful creed;
protecting against uncomprehending flesh.

Men to her required pattern
did not occur.
Marrying one, she was frigid;
could have sent him mad
but that he was
dedicated against madness.

Leaving him, she went to a far place.
Reversing received values. Blasting known territory
she went; in bitterness withering; in mockery smashing;
religious rotes never before questioned all now rejected.
Starting from nothing she began a search; a far way
searching chaos, the initial explosion, the chemistry
of processes. 'I know no Creator.'
Despair now was differently huge. No short-cut
to discovery which was a movement
infinitesmally gradual, pain-broken.
Everything was for experiment down the reptile
slope to the slime, the pit.

A new litany: no longer
Tower of Ivory
House of Gold, but
The great entangling in selfish self
The knot in knot
The no-loving
The pervading hate
The blank withholding from fellow-beings
The almost final withdrawal . . .

but that at the lowest fall
old spurned phrases began their incarnation,
took on palpable lineaments of felt truth,
justifying the cliché, *the valley of the shadow;*
the whole of creation groaneth and travaileth.
'I know myself groan of the general groan,
I am a shadow in the shadow, am in that death
which is cleavage of flesh from soul
noncelebrative heritage, Orphic bequest become
a poisoned pulpit system
refusing to affirm the sanctity of body.
I am in that death which negates completion
of the circle to rebirth,
polar to the death which is resurgent, says yes,
choruses paeans to the flesh forever regenerate.'

In the graveyard Ellen and Thomas
long lay under yearly greening trees;
each spring new children ran in fields.

For their daughter no galvanic revelation,
no cataclysmic light, only a slow knowing
of the worth of real control (slow by wracked slow),
discipline proceeding from the inmost out,
not conversely pontificated. Insights come
from such control, and from one other thing,
a special indefinable she came to feel
must be grace — a word, a concept despised
in her jettisoned legacy of values as meaningless

to her spread search; she grew now to salute grace
the unattached gift which led
to some necessary humbleness
some freeing of the web, some opening
towards new receptivity.

No dazzling vision
but a beginning of belief
in the great importance
of believing, hoping, loving
— against odds,
celebrating tenuous evidence,
further intimations
of the possible integral being:
fusion of flesh and spirit,
continuing, even so, the enigma.

Returning, she was not too late.